Grand

Marla Stewart Konrad

Tundra Books

Text and photographs copyright © 2010 by World Vision

All royalties from the sale of this book go to support World Vision's work with children.

Published in Canada by Tundra Books,
75 Sherbourne Street, Toronto, Ontario M5A 2P9

Published in the United States by
Tundra Books of Northern New York,
P.O. Box 1030, Plattsburgh, New York 12901

Library of Congress Control Number: 2009935195

Library and Archives Canada Cataloguing in Publication

Konrad, Marla Stewart
      Grand / Marla Stewart Konrad.
ISBN 978-0-88776-997-9

      1. Grandparents—Juvenile literature. 2. Grandparent and child—Juvenile literature. I. World Vision Canada
II. Title. III. Series: World Vision early readers

HQ759.9.K63 2009   j306.874'5   C2009-902988-X

We acknowledge the financial support of the Government of Canada through the Book Publishing Industry Development Program (BPIDP) and that of the Government of Ontario through the Ontario Media Development Corporation's Ontario Book Initiative. We further acknowledge the support of the Canada Council for the Arts and the Ontario Arts Council for our publishing program.

**ONTARIO ARTS COUNCIL
CONSEIL DES ARTS DE L'ONTARIO**

Printed and bound in China

1 2 3 4 5 6   15 14 13 12 11 10

Photo Credits:

Cover: Jon Warren, Cambodia
Title Page: Lu Fengxian, China
Dedication Page: Sibusisiwe Ndlovu, Zimbabwe

Spreads

Love Me: TL - John Schenk, Romania; BL - Marie Cook, Kenya; TR - Daniel Lopez, Dominican Republic; BR - Corina Suta, Romania
Share Jokes and Stories: TL - Nigel Marsh, Uganda; BL - Philip Maher, Kenya; R - Philip Maher, Uganda
Quiet Time: L - Jon Warren, Zambia; TR - Justin Douglass, Mongolia; BR - Kit Shangpliang, Sri Lanka
Helping in the Garden: TL - Makopano Letsatsi, Lesotho; BL - Wadi Razzouk, West Bank; TR - Sylvia Nabanoba, Uganda; BR - Alyssa Bistonath, South Africa
Doing Chores Together: TL - Robert Coronado, Kenya; BL - Justin Douglass, Mongolia; TR - Jon Warren, Zambia; BR - Karl Grobl, Cambodia
They are Proud of Me: TL - Jon Warren, India; BL - Ani Chitemyan, Armenia; R - Rebecca Lyman, Pakistan
Grandma Loves Animals: L - Alyssa Bistonath, South Africa; TR - Mkama Mwijarubi, Tanzania; BR - Akilulu Kassaye, Ethiopia
I Feel Safe: Jon Warren, Ethiopia
Old but Wise: TL - Ann Birch, Ghana; BL - Mary Kate MacIsaac, Afghanistan; R - Jerry Galea, Vietnam
Depending on Each Other: L - David du Chemin, Uganda; TR - World Vision Photo, Armenia; BR - Jon Warren, India
Isn't it Grand: Laura Runcanu, Romania

For Norrine Ballinger,
and in memory of Herb Ballinger – grandest of all!

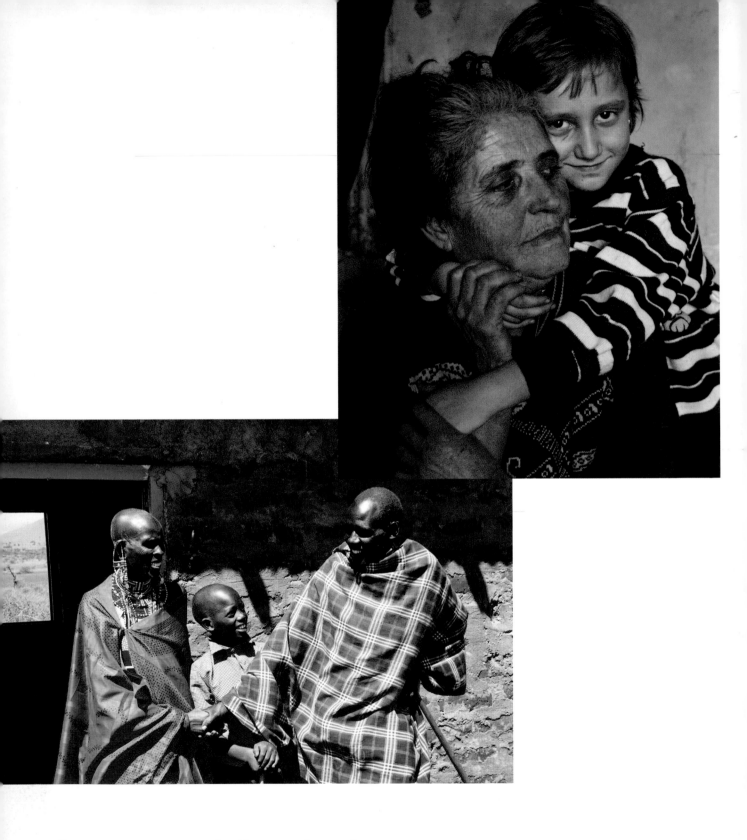

Grandma and Grandpa love me. . . .

And that's really grand!

We share jokes and
stories, and we make
each other laugh.

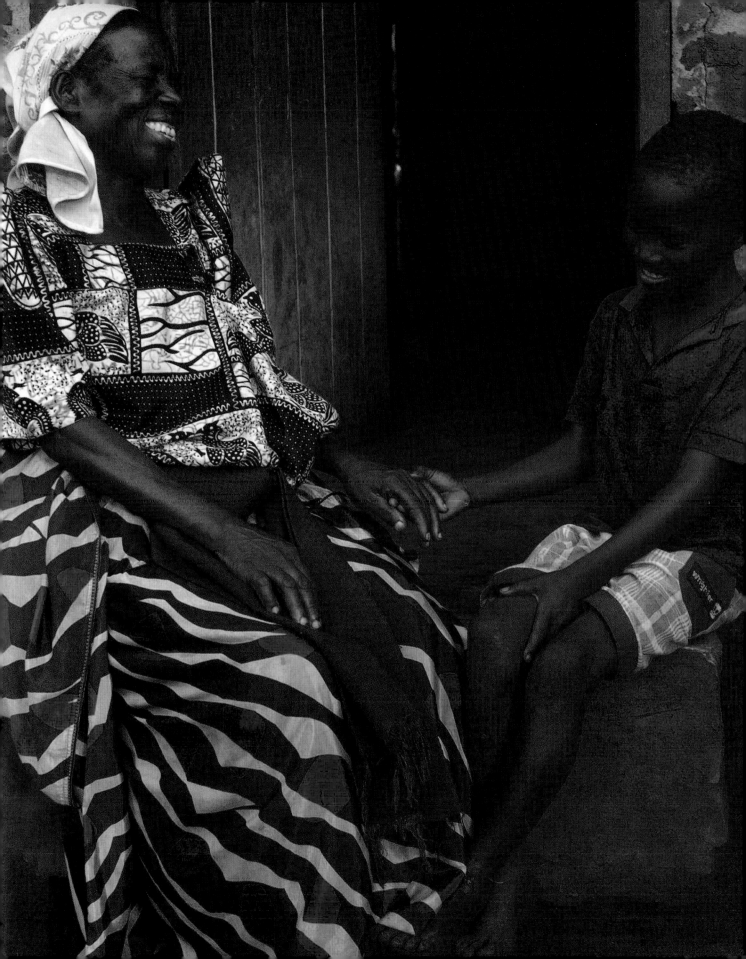

We love to spend quiet time together.

Grandma thinks I'm very clever when I help her in the garden.

Sometimes we like to
do the chores together.

It's grand to know they are so proud of me.

Grandma loves animals
as much as I do!

When I am with Grandpa, I feel safe.

Grandparents might be very old, but they are very wise too.

We depend
on each other.

Isn't that grand!